ASCENDING THE REED

Poems by
Ramson Lomatewama

Library of Congress catalog card number
ISBN 0-935825-01-0

Printed in the U.S.A.
Mirror Images
Flagstaff, Arizona

Acknowledgements
Blue Flute Spring has appeared in SPIRIT OF THE SENSES Journal (1986).

The first edition of ASCENDING THE REED is made possible through the support of the Dr. and Mrs. Dean Nichols Publications Fund, The Heard Museum, Phoenix, Arizona.

* The last line in the poem Lovescape, is taken from the book "Becoming Visible" by Philip Lamantia.

BADGER CLAW PRESS
6693 N. Snowflake Drive
Flagstaff, Arizona 86004

CONTENTS

ASCENDING THE REED

Poems by
Ramson Lomatewama

For Mike

And Jesus said unto him, "Verily I say unto thee,
Today shalt thou be with me in paradise."

St. Luke 23:43

PART I

BIRTH

Young corn breaks ground
showered by rays of the rising sun.

They grow in happiness,
become filled with warmth.

Silky tassles grow long,
like my hair,
in search of new beginnings.

Tomorrow,
itaha taawa
travels the longest day.

With pipe in hand,
we await our elders
who bring the rain.

(Itaha taawa - my uncle, the sun)

UMTOYNAQA

Thundermaker smiles
in the east,
the colors of dawn
on forehead.
Lightning roars
around and around
spinning the ends
of cotton strands.
Wearing abalone
that sparkle and sing
as the rain falls,
he summons the rain.
A ribbon of shells
make sounds of the sea.
His quiet walking
toward noon
pauses
only to spin
thunder from the sky.
When the sun breathes
longer days,
butterfly maidens will
gracefully dance on air,
floating lightly,
sweeping the air
with eagle feathers in hand.

Their feet,
yellow with pollen,
move with delicate strength
over fields of flowers.
Rainbow stands above
a crown of parrot feathers.
Black rain hides
the eyes of butterflies.

At the edge of the field
morning doves
weave flights of cotton.
Moonlight trickles
down this lapis night.

This power of thunder
brings me home.

POOSIW

Poosiw follows the dawn
seeking beauty songs
rolling again and again
in velvet sea-sky.

We close our eyes
and color our songs
with butterfly wings.
We breath mist of life.
We become birds,
We become butterflies,
We become quartz,
We become awakening earth.

We meld our prayers;
paint our thoughts
with sun's warmth
and earth's morning mist.

We carry pollen of purity
above and below creation.
We are the wings of poosiw.

We are westward,
soon to be
song

purity

new life.

SOLSTICE

Winter clouds weep.
Moon paints hazy circle
color of dry grass.
In wandering river,
thin blanket of ice

cracks

floats downstream
over fields of silent stars.

Tamaracks

Cattails

Willows

rooted in the earth;

They look upon lonely ice
quietly drift away.

DREAMING OF EAGLES

You were young
and hungry.

I brought you home.
You were my child.

You lived atop my house.

My mothers washed
your soft white hair.
They gave you names.

In the morning
I watched you
shout out
and spread your wings
to capture rays of the sun.

I heard you call
to all who would listen.
I fed you
and you never hungered.

The moon died many times
before home dance came.
The spirits gave you gifts

awta
yungyapu
tihu

you were happy.

And when I took you down
you weren't afraid.
I prayed for your forgiveness
and you did.

Tomorrow,
you shall return
to our fathers' homes.
When they ask you
from where you came
tell them about your home
where you had many names.
Where you never hungered.

In this way
Shall life go on.
You have never really left us.
You return to life
when your feathers dance in the plaza.

awta - bow (and arrows)
yungyapu - wicker plaque
tihu - katsina doll

WATERFALLS

Glistening water
swept over smooth rocks.
Whirlpools capture moonbeams,
turning light into dark.
Ferns and elderberry
sing childhood songs.

One stem of tall grass
lives alone
away from drops of midnight dew.
Trickles of aged rain
feel their way back
to misty waters.

Gazing at me,
I drop small stones
into calm waters,
and ask,
"Why do I grow old?"
Anxiety twists my mind.

Time passes.

Calm waters return.

I see reality again

One moment of silence
whispers to me -
"There is no time
in reflections."

TURQUOISE NEVER DIES

On sandy slopes
where spotted corn grows,
I sit in the shade
of old-man peach tree.
Looking back,
I see a boy
playing by cool spring water
throwing mud and laughing.
I watch with keen eyes,
his life carve a small stream of childhood
into a river that flows forever.
I watch his hours of laughter,
his moments of tears.
I see his life unfold
like the morning glories
that blossom before the sun.
I watch his dreams
take flight
like the eagle
whose flight proclaims
the marriage of power and grace.
Looking back,
I see why seasons are resurrected;
why life is blind to the passing of time;
why memories are eternal.

I sit here with
the stone in my hand
and the sky above...

and think...
stones crumble
with the passing of time;
skies fade into darkness.
But turquoise never dies.

BLUE FLUTE SPRING

Shallow clear water
falling stars
reflected on ripples
tails of fire
burnished into life *forever.*

Soft green moss
dance along banks
at blue flute spring
swaying
ever so gently.

Drops of rain
make widening circles,
they interweave
and fade into silence.

Paa-atu, the water spider,
rides reflection
of August full moon,
Stars are looking down *pondering.*

Crickets and frogs
gather at waters edge
singing songs of joy.

Desert rose
listens with me
as gray-mist woman
dances
with harvest night.

Velvet shadows lay
with blue flute stones
that rest
and sleep under stream.

Spider woman comes
and listens to chanting water.
Heartbeats echo   within.

I listen
as firefly maiden
sings light
among sumac people.

I listen
as thundercloud fathers
travel from mountain kivas
melting all darkness
with lightning.

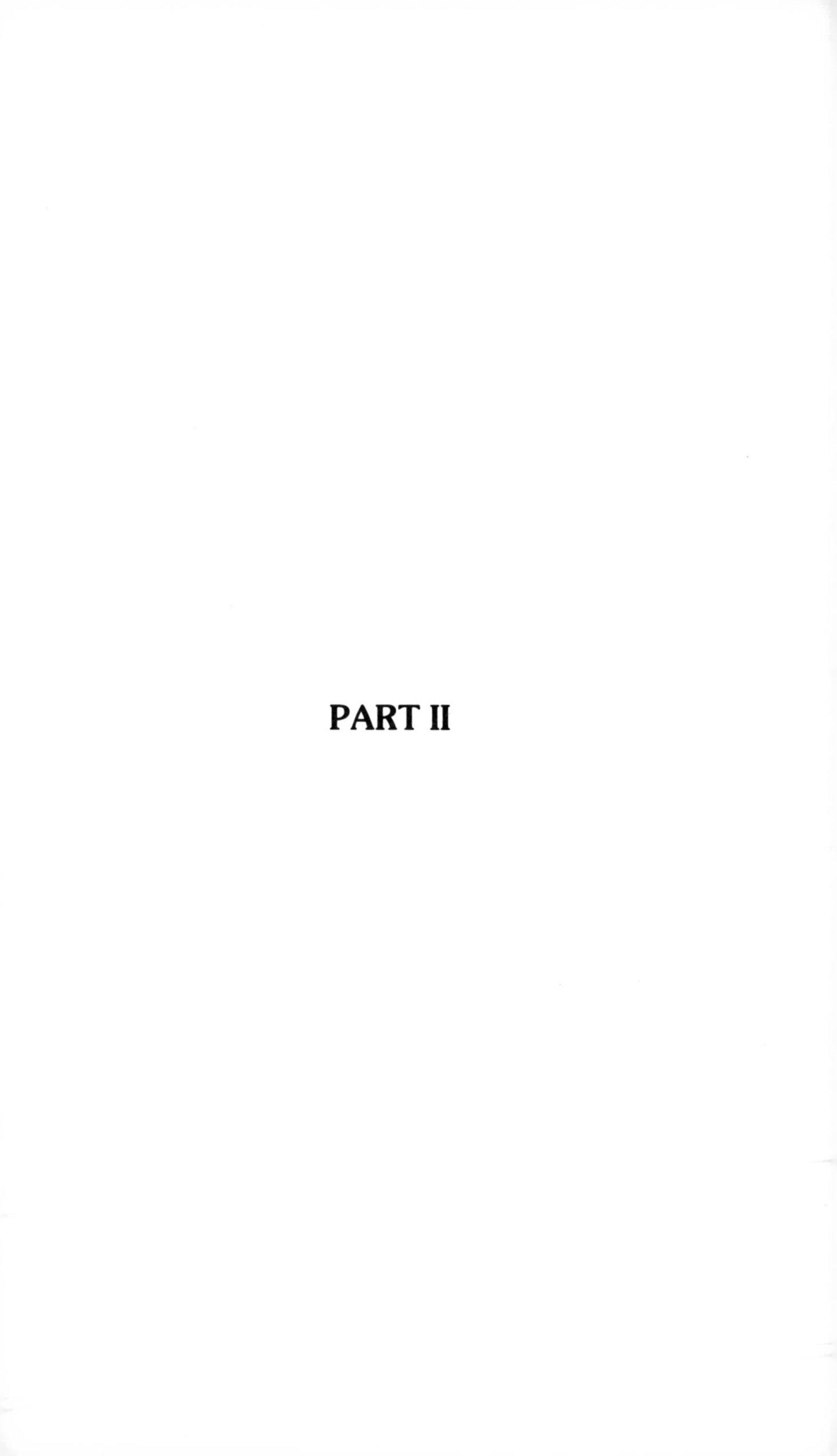

PART II

DESERT ROSE

Desert rose
before my eyes.

Never was it the same in past
nor will it ever be in future.

Once
and only once

will this scarlet blossom be
as I see it now.

Even now,
this moment

has come and gone.
What have we done with it?

What have we done
with all those moments?

Moments like these must be lived.
present is only illusion,

There is only past and future.

Let us make our moments
our existence together
a song of six directions.

A song so beautiful,
that spirit of endless space
will come and say

Never was it same in past
nor will it ever be in future.

ZEPHYRS

Swirling people
Carry the world around
Around
Drifting slowly
Twisting sumac.
Grasses toss their heads
And pick up grains of sand.

Outside
Tumbleweeds
Look for shady corners.

You sit in the sun.
You weave beauty
Moist with rainbow colors.
A part of you
Embraced with black yucca.

I am carried aloft
As I watch your hands
Weave a path
For colors to follow.

I see myself
Looking down at me
And me
Looking up.

My thoughts
Weightless
Circling the air
Ever so slowly
With your thoughts.

We radiate
All directions at once.

I float
On the warmth of your eyes.

When the stars come out
You and I
Will dance
On the milky way.

LAUGHING

Rushing through aspen hills
you come back laughing,

singing.

Leaves of summer
shimmer
a sleepy
green,
when sunlight
bathes
on mountain slopes.

You laugh along
the same road the wind travels.

Bluebirds glide
among ascending spruce
chasing your laughter.

Chipmunks hide
secrets of summer that lay
buried in rumors
of fallen leaves.

You laugh
behind old-man oak
whose back is bent
in wonder.
And dancing stream
mirrors your beauty.

Lizard cracks
dry brown leaves,
darting east   west
*   north   south*
watching the rainbow
race the sun.

Hummingbird sips
the sweet nectar,
drops a feather
into the arms
of lovers.

You,
who we call life,
forever come back

laughing.

SONG TO THE BREEZE

When you whisper
to four-color corn,
they laugh.
You make them laugh.
We walk among corn children,
caressing tender young leaves.
We help corn maidens
tease the ground;
tickle the earth,
when their leaves,
green and slender
stroke the sleeping sand.
Sand laughs,
and swirls away.
You help the sand run away.
You watch me laugh
when I hear them laugh.
My song to you
is filled with laughter.
Can you hear the song?
Do you feel the song?
Can you hear?
Can you hear?

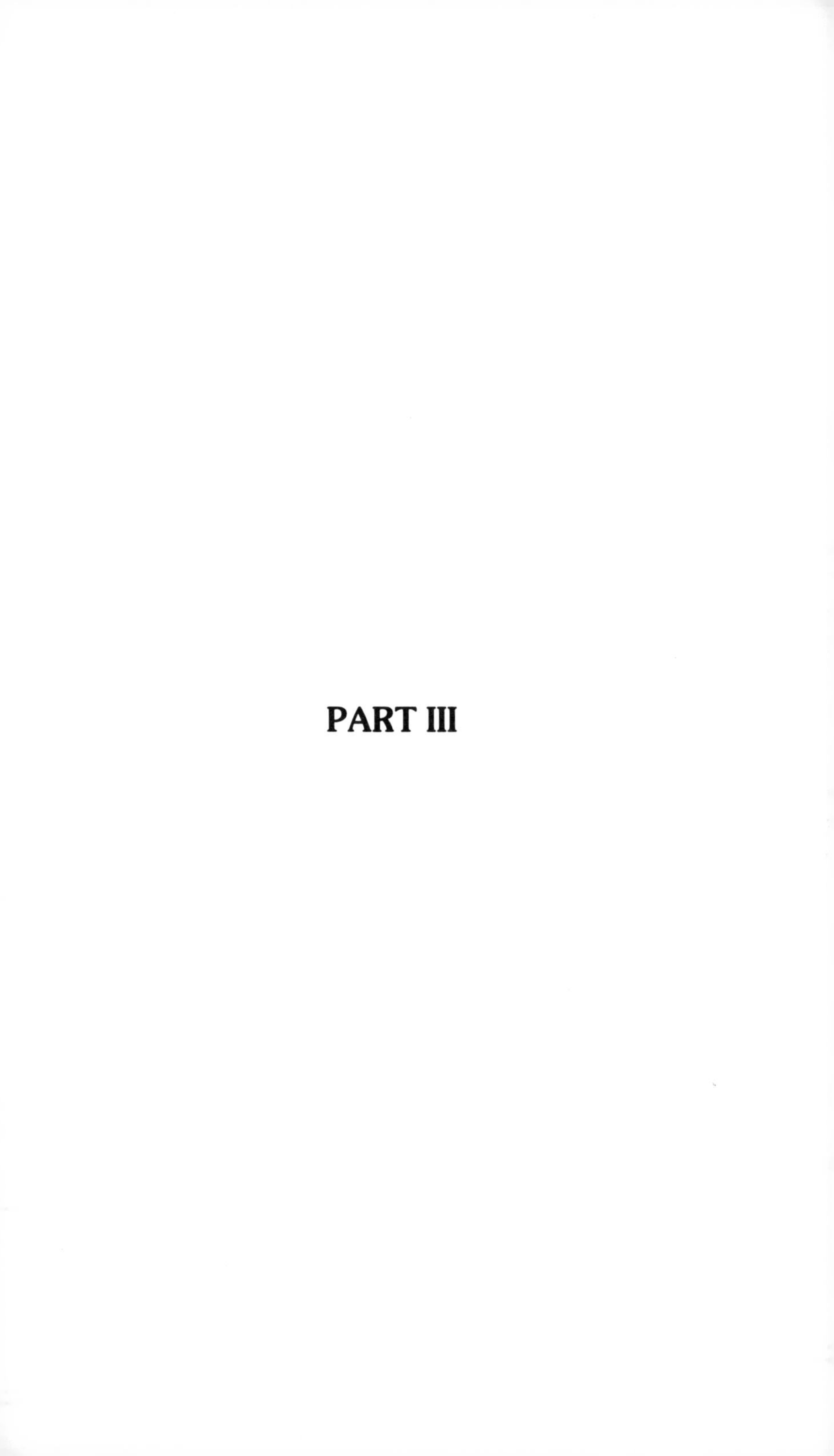

PART III

SKY

The dawn
appears,

waking up
the desert.
Again, I

wonder why the
horizon is
so far away.
Only one person

knows why the caged bird
sings. Would you know why,
if one day, the sky
ceased to love the land?
This land, far from home.

BARREN

Under the rolling hills,
a grave of silent crickets
turn away from
the wandering soul.
Stars appear
one by one.
Our mother
turned barren
with the coming of Kyaamuya.
Tonight, the moon hides her face.
A man and a woman
walk hand in hand,
reflecting the past
with tears and whispers.
The dark trail
leads to the home of ants;
There is no life within.
Tonight,
a wandering bear child
bleeds at the paws.
Far to the north,
a desparate pack of stray dogs
trample the graves
that lie under the rolling hills.
A home atop the mesa
is barren.
Tonight,
The streets of Delhi
are trampled by the millions.

THE PREACHER

I turn and look.

Over my shoulder,
a sign wavers.

white faded abandoned.

REVIVAL

Fifty feet of dirt road
(too far to walk...)
A circus tent
flaps in the wind
shaking off dust

and obscurity.

It is empty,
but for rows
of rusty folding chairs.

Can religion survive
at Tuuwanasavi?

Nothing grows here.
not sage.
not green pasture.
not even faith.

Would it be different
if I were standing at the pulpit?

DEAD SOLDIERS

I've talked to them
under the tall dark oak trees,

many times.

I've thrown dead soldiers
out my car window;
watched them bounce
across the yellow line;
watched
as they faded with the passing of summer.

At times,
I held them in my arms.
Cried,
when they brought back memories
of my father.

Together
we found our way around Hotevilla;
dug into pockets for coins;
brought home scars and bleeding hearts.

I killed my last soldier years ago,
and look at those who still fight their wars.

They
still knock at my door.

Sometimes, I answer.

KING OF THE...

With cigarette sagging
from lips of hunger,
the hunched-back man
in checkered shirt
reaches for another match.
Two dead ones lay at his feet.
He stares into space,
oblivious to reality
around him.
His alley-stained pants
testify a life
of loneliness and despair.
The freezing wind
rushes upon him
and slaps his face,
mocking his very existence.

In a moment of unleased anger,
he curses the world
and every disbeliever.
With tears running down his face
he looks up at a smog-filled heaven,
and cries out,
"My God, my God.
Why hast thou forsaken me?!"
Falling against the black snow,
he weeps and finds comfort
in a bottle of cheap wine.
Three dead ones lay at my feet
crucified,
on the streets of Chicago.

A POEM FOR GRANDMAS

One life undisturbed.
One blade of grass.
One fragment of sky.

Fullness of dawn
sparkles a beauty
the color of peacocks.

The old woman,
curled against White Cafe
is dreaming,

turning years
over and over,
waiting for a life
that left her far behind.

She drowns herself
in rivers of desolation,
and comes up for air, hung over.

Her wrinkled times
drunken day after day after day,
blend into butterfly dreams.

Her childhood
lies half buried
in dirty snow.

On Sunday mornings,
she chants under a bridge
three worlds ago,
certain
that her words
have traveled
light years upon light years.

Listen.
and you can hear
the rain whisper

"Old woman
wake up
and come back home."

"Old woman,
come back
to one life
undisturbed."

EVENING THOUGHTS

How sad they must be
when they go home at sunset.
To see us as we are,
when we, who call ourselves Hopi
have no respect
for ourselves
nor for life itself.
They have known this.
And they are everywhere
watching us.
They are the evergreen trees
that defy the harsh winter;
they are the clouds
upon whom gravity has no power;
they are the eagles
who ride the silent winds;
they are the old
and the new;
they are life.
they know two worlds,
theirs and ours,
and no sin goes unseen.
How sad
kachinas must be
when they go home
at sunset.

RAIN

Cloud priests
come forth
to our fields of corn
who thirst
at tuuwanasavi

Rain priest from north
dressed in the color of the sun
come
look down upon purple cactus blossoms
where butterflies paint
gentle breath of windbreaker moon

Rain priest from west
adorned in the beauty of the sky
come
listen to grandmother spiderwoman
weave legends deep into night

Rain priest from south
cloaked in the color of warmth
come
walk across the desert sand
taste rising mist of roasted corn

Rain priest from east
draped in the beauty of snow
come
breathe rain upon your children
rest in the branches of evergreen trees

Come
for these are the signs of life

Cloud priests
come forth

Our way of life is slowly dying

And we are thirsty

AFTER ARMAGEDDON

A crystal palace
floating
on wild swirling clouds
suspended
in a red room without walls.

Iridescent streaks of lightning
lick
the heavy-breathing stars of old.

Dead raven soldiers
align themselves like sardines
on this fiery floor of hell.

My angels defy death
stabbing the lies of all mankind
laughing themselves
into funnels of mass hysteria.

A mighty fist of smoke
chokes a land of freedom
spreading the message of death
spreading our love to destroy.

Dance with me.

Dance around insane fires.

Around eternal blasphemy.

Listen.

Listen to mothers burning
and fathers drowning
in the sea of koyaanisqatsi.

Chant up the final day
with radioactive resonance.
Let the children born
and unborn
watch
the gourd of ashes fall

down

down

down.

Let it be known to all
that pass between
my serpentine fingers
that I will squeeze
those succulent dreams
out of your god-forsaken souls
and cast you down
with the cynical smile
of Lucifer himself.

We are the power
We are the glory
We are the kingdom
after Armageddon

forever.

KOYAANISQATSI

In timber and time alone
I saw in a parting sea
a thousand golden chariots.

They stormed past the future,
taking with them
nothing but the blood
of children lost.

I shot a cloud of blue,
heard the scream
of my own sweat,
heard the voice
of history shout

"Damned are the souls of suicide!"

"Damned are the makers of war!"

Now I run through a tunnel of death,
feeling only the terror
whipping against my face,

        and yours.

I dream realities
among the tall white aspens.
We stand under a thick black sky.

Let us watch
a thousand golden chariots
trample the roads
of our exploding
frenzied
minds.

DRUNK WITH RAGE

You judge above cruel insanity,
Among flute music sons. Laughing
Through dusty justice, you crack
Abundant blue, and wound us.

Black juice of lust - smooth
Enchanted ooze - comes rushing to
Plunge uprooted agonies into tumbling
Pools of subdued anger.

Undefined moods loosen hungry fanatics
Who uncover sublunar madness.

PART IV

WINDOWS

Standing here
protected from raging winds.

Staring out this wall of glass
I ponder golden sand
laced with aggressive snow.

The mesa across the valley
draped in white
sleeps under a veil of gray sky.
Winter clouds drift by.
(George Winston plays Autumn behind me.)

I wander through a maze of music.
my breath mingles
with my ancestors'.
Winter winds
burn my freezing face.
I am
Standing on mesa edge
shouting like juniper and pinyon
in defiance of aging winter;
Listening for thunder in the valley
among sand dunes and sumac;
watching the approaching snow
as it comes charging across the field;
tasting the essence of winter;
living the spirit of earth below;

being a part of this world,
being a part of this life,

indescribable.

AN EVENING AT WINDY POINT
For Christopher Jay

The sound of suizen
lingers over a valley of sand.
Desert shadows grow in silence.
Clouds float in flames of sunset.
The man, sitting at the edge
brings music to Windy Point.
Below,
juniper and pinon trees listen.
Smooth bamboo songs
touch the face of summer.
There are no monastary walls here,
Only the music,
the man,
the spirit.

SOUTHWEST COFFEE HOUSE
Durango, Colorado

Dark dusty Durango sky
clouds bustin rain
main street on a rush.
Here's where I'm at —
People throwin glances
all kinds of people
they smile
they stare
they glare.
Bikers n bikes
outside the Maverick Saloon.
Horse drawn carriage
black with the fringe on top
loaded down
with camera totin'
dead skin men
in bermuda shorts.
Ain't seen one black yet.

A far different place than Hotevilla.
Ain't many blacks there either.

MBTA AQUARIUM

Mind-body-soul descend
vibration runs infinity
rubberhard rails
make my palm turn black
grumbling machines
echo full circle
 step
  slide
   down
to a cold dark hell

  vanish under lakes of concrete

    DEEP

    DOWN DEEP
inna belly of a snake

I sit and stare
at cold steel
running side by side
into a gloom far beyond
Salt water soaks
underground air
voices crash
back and forth
half-empty beer
sits abandoned
waiting for the final swallow.
here,
time doesn't travel

    The tunnel rumbles

     LOUDER

     AND LOUDER

double doors
ear split open

I step inside
My body rattles
a death song

beats to the rhythm
of a railroad track
we crawl through years
and years of graffiti

FASTER and FASTER

through FLAshes and FLAshes of LIGHT and DARK!

FASTER and FASTER

THE SPEED OF LIGHT!

FASTER AND FASTER!

MINUTES MELT INTO MILES!

AND MILES AND MILES!

My brain sizzles
HOTTER AND HOTTER

FASTER AND FASTER!

there is no end...

BOSTON STREETS

New England days
filled with salty air;
beaches of white
stretched up and down
as far as imagination;
pieces of shell trapped in wet sand;
strands of seaweed
swell in and out with the tide.

I sit and watch the mist
blend water and sky,
feel the gray afternoon
settle down on
a cemetary by the sea.
Loneliness, my only friend.
We sit on a park bench
and watch shadows crawl
up walls of steely glass.
I rub my hands,
polish warmth
into my palms.

The fire of sunset burns in the west.
I walk past a Boston home
and listen to the screams
of a man and a woman.
Outside,
he sits on the wooden steps,
crying.
I see the smokey breath of sorrow
in the soft light of the moon.

I stop to watch
those almost forgotten days,
but that was years ago.
This is now.

Who am I?
to wrap this child in warmth;
to show him that love still exists.
To tell him that, I too,
cried on a wooden porch so long ago.
But this world we share
will not allow us to share.
We are mirrors
one for the other.

A single tear runs down.
Far behind me,
a child cries.

SHADOWS
For Philip and Nancy

Watching lamplight through tired eyes
I listen for echoes of childhood
feeling silky waves flow within me.

Images form
and re-form.

I sit in silence, watching my thoughts.
The old chair creaks
at the slightest movement of my feet.
And I fall
deeper
and deeper
into a well
of light
and dark.
I could hear
the pounding of ironwood
upon a loom of dreams.

...and blood filled my head.

Last night, I had a dream
of looking down upon a man
sitting upon a rainbow halo
surrounded by
earth
water
fire
and air.

I stood next to this man
whose black hair was the rain.
He gazed at the earth
and made it warm.
He was a breather of clouds
and sweet aroma
of mountain tobacco
swirled into heaven.

He looked up
through eyes of obsidian
and spoke:

"Once
clouds came together
sat around
their mountain altar
chanting
as the cresent moon
faded into a lace-wing sunset.
Once
the moon drank nectar
giving birth
to winter nights.
The snow children
glittered with innocence
and danced.
Once
Elk people
chanted medicine songs
and rain fell
upon the arms
of blue spruce maidens.
Once
younger sister
fire-tender
breathed life
within the holy clouds
who were born
of burning tobacco.
Once
the shadow of man
had life of its own
loving the earth
being faithful to the creator
accepting all obstacles
working around them
respecting
and reflecting
the law of the son
and the sun.

Then
I found myself in a world of light,
swam through the tail of a comet.
I could see infinity
before my eyes.
I was beyond tomorrow
floating upon
misty pulsations
of time and space
carried by mystic waves
from star to star
being immersed in seas
of lucid
and undefiled love
letting my soul escape
the plane of human sensation

becoming now

becoming free

becoming visible!

JADE

I wander in a field of jade.
I linger at the gate of death.

Shadows trickle around me.

flickering ashes
send gentle swirls of orange

up to the hungry clouds.

Winter moon chants down a light song.

At midnight
the ivory shore
suckles the halo of gray ocean mist.

Swaggering and drunk
I wander empty headed.

Forty-five days
since I left the gray walls.

The man who would be my father
came to me.
The sun was high again.

Tonight
she cries,
filling lakes with sorrow.

No one feels her pain,
except me;

wishing
and wanting

of those smooth nights together.

LOVESCAPE

Brittle summer evening,
cliffs and canyons
scorched by crimson sky.
Darkness becomes master.
I gaze into mystery fire.
My soul melts
becoming cloistered
in dancing flames.
And after time unknown
My eyes drink
the glowing embers.

It was then
that I saw her,
bathing in fires
of all time.
She pondered antiquity,
and dust of her memories
stirred once more
and turned to streaks of lightning.
Then
with beauty of life
she spoke to the night
and me.
I am the daughter of nature
and I reflect intense desires
of you
and me.
My eyes
and the blue-gray light
of the weeping moon
stroked her soft and tender face.
She smiled
not at me,
but at the lonely moon.
She consoled the moon
with her smile,
and I fell deeper and deeper
in love.

Brittle summer morning
cliffs and canyons
soothed by crimson sky.
Dawn becomes master.
Splinters of burnt offerings
lay about
like shattered pottery.
I held the future in my hands.
Last night
I was so close to you
I watched your eyes
dance with stars.

I watched you
caress the lonely moon.
I heard the comfort
of your celestial heart.
I felt your breath
running with mine.
And when you spoke to me in the night,
stars watched.
All universe ceased to exist,
except you
and I
together.

PONDERING TOMORROWS

for Jessica, Stephanie, Caryl, Ellen, and Justin

Days follow days.
Rainbows born in rain.
I ponder dreams.
I teach them
to make angels in the snow.
I watch her spin black yucca
around clouds of yellow,
clouds of blue,
clouds of red.
I listen to stories
as I weave a cloud of white.
And you,
who came from within,
a still path is before you.
Your breath remains pure
as the purple light of dawn.
all of you will sing
the long life of badger.
I shall be in your song.

LAST SONG

Life dances
in the womb
of our village.

Spirits of long ago
sing on purified sand.

The songs of beauty and life
seep down into the earth.

Rattling down the rain,
they sing of happiness.

Gourds of thunder
rumble under the song.

They dance one final prayer.
It is time for the last song.

Somewhere far away,
Spruce tree people
listen for rain songs.

Somewhere far away,
white clouds and rainbows
listen for one final prayer.

And here,
people of the fourth world
listen for the last song.

It is here
that we part with the breaking of branches.

HUNGER

Crow
hidden by juniper
spying from trecherous cliffs

aches with hunger.

Taste of sweet roasted corn
fondling my mind.
Still

many hours before sunrise.

Neither the crow
nor myself

find satisfaction.

We wait for tomorrow,

with wings,

with pen.

WITHOUT DREAMS

Without dreams
we would have no faith
in the clouds
that bring the summer rain.

Without dreams
we would not sing
to the corn
to make them happy.

Without dreams
we would have
no reason to live.